THE BOOK OF
EXTREMES

● ● ● ● ● ● ● ● ● ● ● ● ● ●

Published for
Tesco Stores Limited
by Brilliant Books Ltd
84-86 Regent Street
London W1R 6DD

First published 1998

Copyright © 1998 Brilliant Books Ltd
Printed by Cambus Litho Ltd, Scotland
Reproduction by Vision Reproductions

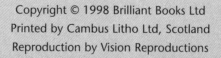

THE BOOK OF
EXTREMES

· · · · · · · · · · · · · · · · · · · ·

Written by
Norris McWhirter

CONTENTS

EXTREME

PEOPLE

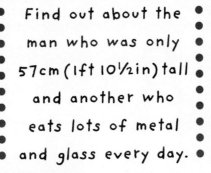

Find out about the
man who was only
57cm (1ft 10½in) tall
and another who
eats lots of metal
and glass every day.

THE TALLEST AND SHORTEST

Just think of being 1.83m (6ft) tall on your eighth birthday. And by the time you are 12½ years old you have grown to 2.13m (7ft).

The only boy in the world ever to really know what this felt like was Robert Wadlow of Alton, Illinois, USA.

He towered over his father, the city's mayor, who was 1.80m (5ft 11in). By the age of ten, Robert could carry him, like a baby, up the front stairs of the family home – with no trouble at all!

Two doctors, Dr Charles and Dr MacBryde, took a great interest in Robert and recorded that by the time he was 16¾ years old he measured 2.43m (8ft).

Apart from having to sleep diagonally in a large double bed, he was barely able to get in and out of a car. But the biggest problems happened when he went outside for a walk. Drivers would slow right down so that they could get a good look at the unbelievable giant. And instead of keeping their eyes on the road, the drivers in the following cars would also be gawping. The result was often a horrible and very expensive crunch!

EXTREME MEASURES The last measurement ever taken of Robert Wadlow was on 27 June 1940, when he was only 23mm (⁹/₁₀ in) short of 2.74m (9ft). He died on 15 July 1940 as a result of gangrene, caused by his poorly fitting leg supports.

TRUE GIANTS

True, perfectly proportioned giants are very rare. William Bradley (right) was England's biggest giant, standing at 2.36m (7ft 9in). The Scotsman, Angus Macaskill, born in 1823, also grew to 2.36m (7ft 9in). He could hold a 50.8kg (112lb) weight from his middle finger, with his arm held out at right angles, for more than ten minutes!

Growing facts

- Most people stop growing in their late teens, but Robert Wadlow was still growing fast after his 21st birthday. He was consuming 8,000 calories a day, nearly four times the intake of the average man, and he was still quite thin!

1.83m (6ft) TALL ON HIS EIGHTH BIRTHDAY!

If you find it hard to imagine being 1.83m (6ft) tall on your eighth birthday, think what it must have been like for Gul Mohammed of New Delhi, in India. On 19 July 1990, when Gul was 33, he was examined by doctors at a hospital. He was measured at 57cm (1ft 10½in) in height – making him the shortest known living person. He may even have been the shortest person of all time. His weight was just 17kg (2 stone 9½lb). Unfortunately, Gul died at the end of 1997.

The shortest known woman was Pauline Musters, known as 'Princess Pauline'. At the age of nine she weighed only 1.5kg (3lb 5oz) and was 55cm (1ft 9⅔in) tall. She hardly grew after that and was measured at 61cm (2ft) after she died in 1895.

VERTICALLY CHALLENGED
Gul Mohammed is the shortest known person of all time.

57cm (1ft 10½in) TALL!

ACROMEGALIC GIANT

A BIG NAME Even the signature of Robert Wadlow, reproduced here at its actual size, was unusually large.

People such as Robert Wadlow are not true giants – their height is out of proportion to the size of their hearts. Because their hands and feet grow so large, doctors call them 'acromegalics' – from the Greek words *akron*, meaning 'extremity', and *megas*, meaning 'large'. Such people also have very large tongues. Their condition is caused by an excess of growth hormone, which causes the hands, feet and facial features to carry on growing, even after other bones in the body are unable to grow any more. Except for a brief time, when they are about 13, acromegalic giants are never very strong.

If you can find a long tape measure, try measuring Robert's height against a wall, perhaps in your school gym – the ceilings in your home are probably not high enough!

HANDS LIKE FEET On his 21st birthday, 'Big Bob' weighed just over 222kg (35 stone). His hands were particularly huge – the distance from the base of his palm to the top of his middle finger was 32.4cm (12³/₄in). His arm-span was also enormous – at 2.88m (9ft 5³/₄in)! His shoes, the biggest ever, were 47cm (18¹/₂in) long – equivalent to a size 37!

Hand-print of a giant

A BIG HAND – 32.4cm (NEARLY 13in) LONG

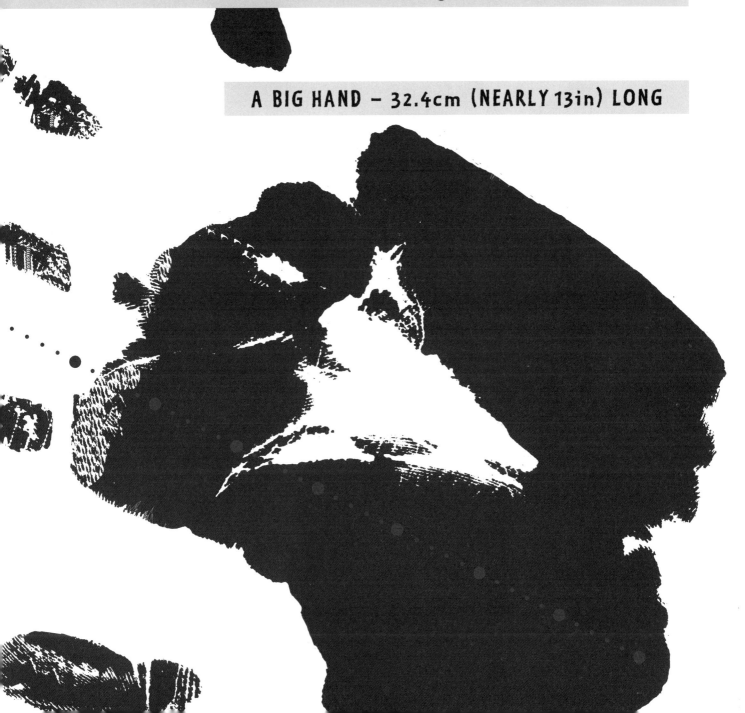

A WEDDING TO REMEMBER

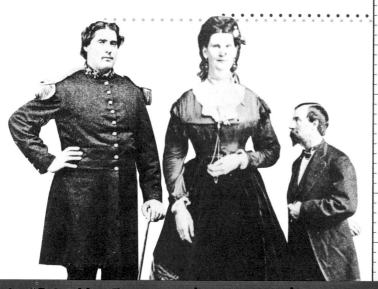

- When they married at
- Seyssinet-Pariset, France,
- on 14 April 1990, Fabien
- Pretou, 1.88m (6ft 2in),
- and Natalie Lucius, 94cm
- (3ft 1in) tall, became the
- married couple with the
- largest height difference.

A GROOM OF 2.20m (7ft 2¾in) AND A BRIDE OF 2.27m (7ft 5½in)

TALL ORDERS Martin van Buren Bates and Anna Hanen Swan had a combined height of 4.47m (14ft 8in), dwarfing the clergyman who was 1.78m (5ft 10in).

The most spectacular wedding ceremony on record took place in London in 1871. The scene was at the altar of St Martin's-in-the-Field on the east side of London's famous Trafalgar Square. Although the bridegroom, an American named Martin van Buren Bates (1845-1919), stood 2.20m (7ft 2¾in), he was overshadowed by his Canadian bride, Anna Hanen Swan (1846-1888). Said to be 2.46m (8ft 3in), she in fact measured 2.27m (7ft 5½in). This tallest ever bridal couple made the officiating clergyman look like a midget! The couple later had two babies – a daughter of 8.16kg (18lb) in 1871 and a son weighing 10.77kg (23lb 12oz), born in 1879. Unfortunately, neither child lived for very long.

BIG FAMILIES AND BIG PEOPLE

Huge families are quite common in some countries. In Victorian times, 150 years ago, many people had as many as 15 brothers and sisters, even in Great Britain. However, a great number of babies at that time did not live to reach their first birthday.

The all-time champion mother was Madame Feodor Vassilyev of the Russian town of Shuya. She had 16 pairs of twins, seven sets of triplets and four sets of quadruplets, making a grand total of 69, without any single births at all. In 1782, the Empress Catherine the Great insisted that the entire family was brought to the Imperial Court, so that she could personally count them. They arrived in a convoy of farm carts. Amazingly, 67 of the 69 children, born between 1725 and 1765, all survived beyond infancy.

IMAGINE – 68 BROTHERS AND SISTERS!

The greatest weight ever recorded for any human was 635kg (100 stone) in the case of the American Jon Brower Minnoch (1941-83). A former taxi driver, he became a taxi dispatcher until he could no longer fit into his booth. He lost over 419kg (66 stone) after two years in hospital, but had to be readmitted after putting on a staggering 89kg (14 stone) in one week!

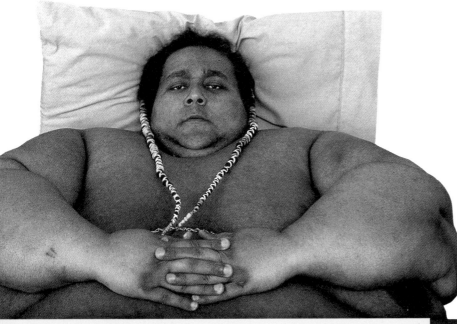

WAIST NOT The waist of Walter Hudson (left) of New York, USA, was a little more than 3m (10ft 11in).

TOPPING THE SCALES AT 545kg (85 STONE)

THE LONGEST LIVING HUMAN

AGE OLD Jeanne Louise Calment holds her age written on card on 19 February 1995, just before her 121st birthday.

GREAT EVENTS OF A LIFETIME

Over the past 122 years, the world has changed more in a shorter period of time than ever before. Here are some of the landmarks that Jeanne Calment lived through.

1876 – one year old
The first telephone call is made.

1885 – 10 years old
The first car, invented by Gottlieb Daimler, takes to the roads. Its top speed is 13km/h (8mph).

1903 – 28 years old
The Wright brothers fly the first powered aircraft.

1925 – 50 years old
The first television picture flickers into life in Soho, London.

1939 – 64 years old
World War II breaks out.

1945 – 70 years old
The Americans drop an atom bomb on Hiroshima, Japan, taking the world into the nuclear age.

1963 – 88 years old
American President John F Kennedy is assassinated.

1969 – 94 years old
Man lands on the Moon.

The most competitive record of all is, quite simply, staying alive. After all, there are now nearly 6,000 million people on earth, almost all of whom are trying to survive for as long as they can. In a hostel in Arles, in southern France, lived the most durable of the 64,000 million humans ever known to have lived. This French woman, Jeanne Louise Calment, was born on 21 February 1875 and reached the extraordinary age of 122 years 164 days. But on 4 August 1997, her strong heart had finally had enough – after beating more than four billion times.

The man with the longest nails

It has been claimed that the loudest ever human voice belonged to the 2.29m (7ft 6in) American giant, Mills Darden (1798-1857). Local people said his bellow could be heard over a mile away.

Shridhar Chillal of India last cut the fingernails of his left hand in 1952. The thumbnail is 1.4m (4ft 7in), the first fingernail 1.09m (3ft 7in), the second fingernail 1.17m (3ft 10in), the third fingernail 1.25m (4ft 1in) and the fourth fingernail 1.22m (4ft) long. He cuts the nails of his right hand, so that he is able to perform everyday tasks. But Shridhar still finds it hard to tie shoe-laces and his nails, which are still growing, have become very difficult to clean!

A THUMBNAIL MEASURING 1.4m (4ft 7in)

NAILED At the end of March 1997, the length of Shridhar Chillal's five nails on his left hand added together came to 6.12m (20ft 1in).

SUPER RICH AND SUPER CLEVER

The American oil man, John Paul Getty, once said: "If you can count your millions, you are not a billionaire." Today, 30 years later, it could be said: "If you can count your billions, you're not the world's richest man."

One of two contenders for this title is the 42-year-old ruling Sultan of Brunei, Sir Muda Hassanal Bolkiah Mu'izzaddin Waddaulah.

As head of both the state and government, he can add billions of Brunei dollars to his personal fortune from his country's huge oil and gas reserves. His fortune is estimated to be worth more than £20 billion (£20,000 million), the interest on which would give him more than £20 million a week!

The Sultan lives in the world's largest residential palace. It contains 1,788 rooms with 257 lavatories. If he slept in a different room each night, it would take him four years, ten months and two weeks before he would have to sleep in the same room twice. Inside the garage he keeps 150 of the world's most expensive cars.

BIG BUCKS The Sultan of Brunei could give every man, woman and child in Britain more than £300 and still be one of the world's richest men.

Bill Gates, founder of the computer company Microsoft, is the richest businessman in the world with a personal fortune estimated to be at least $34 billion (£20.6 billion).

WORTH A STAGGERING $34 BILLION

BRAINS AND BEAUTY

THE FACES OF FORTUNE Kate Moss (top left) and Naomi Campbell are among the highest paid models. Together they are allegedly worth more than £31 million.

DON'T GET UP FOR UNDER $10,000

- Croydon-born superwaif Kate Moss is reported to have taken French citizenship for tax purposes. Her contract with Calvin Klein alone earns her £2.5 million a year and she is now estimated to be worth at least £15 million.

CLEVER CLOGS

One of the cleverest people of all time was the Nobel Prize winner and physicist Albert Einstein (1879-1955). He is best known for his theory of relativity, ($E=mc^2$ where E=energy, m=mass and c=the speed of light), which eventually led to the creation of the first atom bomb.

Ganesh Sittampalam, above, however, is the youngest person to have passed an A level, getting a grade A in both Mathematics and Further Mathematics in June 1988, at the age of nine.

STRANGE EATING HABITS

Michel Lotito from Grenoble in France, known as 'Monsieur Mangetout', found by chance that he could literally eat anything. He has been eating 900g (2lb) of metal and glass a day since 1959 and, as the years have gone by, his feats have become more and more extreme. His unique diet has included 18 bicycles, 15 supermarket trolleys, seven television sets, a computer, a coffin, a pair of skis and even a Cessna light aircraft!

QUITE A MOUTHFUL Michel Lotito tucks into part of a car. When the Guinness Book of Records presented 'Monsieur Mangetout' with a plaque, he started to eat it!

WARNING!
DO NOT TRY THIS AT HOME

HARD TO SWALLOW

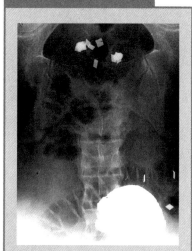

His own doctor failed to persuade 'Monsieur Mangetout' to change his diet, while British doctors thought he was a fake. When he came to Britain, the doctors tried to catch him out. They put him in front of a scanner to prove that he was a fraud. But to their horror, the X-rays confirmed that he really was swallowing the chunks of metal! And he seemed to enjoy every mouthful.

EXTREME

EXPLOSIONS
AND DISASTERS

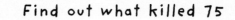

Find out what killed 75
million people and what made
a wave 524m (1,720ft) high!

EXTREME EARTHQUAKES

Earthquakes occur in many of the world's 192 countries. No other natural phenomenon can be as destructive over so large an area in so short a time. Earthquakes can topple buildings and cause landslides and mudslides. They can also cause huge sea waves. In July 1998, an earthquake resulted in a wave which tragically killed 4,000 people after it hit Papua New Guinea's coast.

In 23 centuries of recorded history, only two people have ever been killed because of an earthquake in Britain. In the reign of the first Queen Elizabeth on 6 April 1580, an apprentice, Thomas Grey, and Mabel Everett, a 13-year-old girl, were walking past Temple Church in London at 6.00pm. Suddenly there was a tremor and debris and slates fell from the church's roof, killing both the unfortunate children.

QUAKE SHAKE

The Earth's crust is made up of giant continental plates. Earthquakes usually occur where these plates meet. When one plate pushes below another, it sends shock waves through the ground. Earthquakes can start 300km (190 miles) below the Earth's surface. The postcard, above, shows the result of the 1906 quake in San Francisco. The city lies on the San Andreas fault where two plates meet.

THE POWER OF NATURE

GREAT SHAKES Many of San Francisco's roads collapsed in the 1989 quake. Amazingly, only 24 people were killed.

Seismic shocks

The worst earthquake in history occurred in China in the province of Shensi in 1556. The earthquake lasted for nearly two hours and destroyed many towns and villages. The area was quite heavily populated and the death toll was 830,000.

Earthquakes are usually measured on the Richter Scale. The more violent the earthquake, the higher the reading will be. The highest ever reading was one of 9.0.

KOBE CATASTROPHE An earthquake which measured 7.2 on the Richter Scale hit Kobe in Japan on 18 January 1995, devastating most of the city. It destroyed buildings, twisted roads and killed more than 5,500 people.

VOLCANIC ERUPTIONS

The loudest and most violent volcanic explosion by far in recent times occurred on 27 August 1883, when the whole of the top of the island of Krakatoa blew off. The island lay between Java and Sumatra in Indonesia, in south-east Asia. Huge chunks of rock flew up to 55km (34 miles) high into the sky. The detonation was so loud that it was heard over one twelfth of the whole Earth's surface, including Australia 4,800 km (3,000 miles) away. The huge sea wave which

RIVERS OF FIRE Mauna Loa, on Hawaii, USA, is the largest active volcano at 4,170m (13,680ft) high, 120km (75 miles) long, and 50km (31 miles) wide.

Natural time bombs

BOOM! The eruption of Krakatoa had the force of 26 atom bombs.

resulted was at least 35m (115ft) high. It hit Java, killing more than 31,000 people on the shore. For two years afterwards, the whole world experienced the most beautiful coloured sunsets – a result of all the volcanic dust in the Earth's atmosphere.

- The most active volcano is Kilauea, on Hawaii, USA. It spews out volcanic ash more than 300m (1,000ft) into the air and erupts about every three weeks for several hours at a time.

Another of the greatest ever eruptions occurred when Tambora, a volcano on the Indonesian island of Sumbawa exploded in April 1815. The total volume of rocks, earth and ash that spewed out was 150-180km³ (36-43 miles³). Ash more than 1cm (½in) thick covered an area six times bigger than England!

Debris darkened the skies, blotting out the Sun for weeks and weeks. This caused a temporary global cooling that made 1816 become known as 'the year without a summer'.

The most violent volcanic event of all happened when Taupo erupted in New Zealand in AD130. It flattened an area three-quarters the size of Wales!

FEARFUL FLOW

Volcanoes are not scattered randomly over the Earth's surface, but occur in belts, especially in the island arcs and ranges of mountains bordering the Pacific Ocean. They are vents in the Earth's crust, usually found on the boundaries between the huge continental plates which cover the Earth. They discharge lava, made up of molten rock, called magma, gases and ash.

TERRIFYING TSUNAMIS

Giant waves should not be called tidal waves, but *tsunamis*. In Japanese *tsu* means 'wild' and *nami* means 'a wave'. Such waves have nothing to do with tides and are usually caused by earthquakes. They race across oceans at speeds of up to 725 km/h (450 mph). The highest recorded *tsunami* occurred on 9 July 1958, when a huge landslide at the head of the narrow fjord-like Lituya Bay in Alaska caused a massive wave. It ripped out all the trees from its steep banks. Surveyors measured the height of the wave by surveying the highest point at which trees had been torn out of the ground and washed out to sea. The figure was an almost unbelievable 524m (1,720ft) – which is much higher than the tallest skyscraper in the world!

- The highest recorded sea wave, caused simply by bad weather, was one of 34m (112ft). It was measured by the terrified crew of the USS *Ramapo* in the western Pacific between the Philippines and the USA, during a 226km/h (140mph) hurricane early in 1933.

CRASH! Atlantic storms seldom cause waves of more than about 15m (49ft) around Britain, but even they can be quite big enough!

Waves of terror

IMAGINE A WAVE 524m (1,720ft) HIGH

LIGHTNING STRIKES

Considering its violence, it is amazing that lightning does not kill more people. A downward flash may measure up to 6km (4 miles) in length and reach a temperature of 16,000°C (28,800°F) – about five times hotter than the surface temperature of the Sun.

Roy Sullivan, a park ranger from Virginia, USA, was struck by lightning seven times. He lost a big toenail and his hair. He suffered burns to his eyebrows, chest, leg and stomach. Eventually, in 1983, he committed suicide!

STORM FORCE

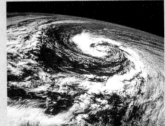

EYE OF THE STORM

A VIOLENT EARTH Forked lightning (left) begins with a faint leader stroke, which takes the route of least resistance to the ground. The massive luminous bolts of lightning are actually 'returns', travelling up from the ground. The Empire State Building (inset, above left) is sometimes struck several times a day at certain times of year. Hurricane Inez (above) hit Florida's coast, near Miami, in 1966 at 160km/h (100mph), causing terrible flooding.

Hurricanes are storms which originate over tropical oceans. As the storm or area of low pressure approaches land, the winds which revolve around it can increase to 290km/h (180mph). Hurricanes usually last about six days, and weaken when they hit the mainland.

- The worst cyclone (or hurricane) in history occurred on 12 November 1970 in Bangladesh. A combination of 240km/h (150mph) winds, flooding and a 15m (50ft) sea wave killed between 300,000 and 500,000 people.

EXPLOSIVE EVENTS

The first atomic bomb used in warfare was dropped on Hiroshima, in Japan, by the Americans at 8.16am on 6 August 1945. Codenamed 'Little Boy', it flattened 10km² (4 miles²) of the city – destroying two-thirds of its buildings and killing 220,000 people.

TESTING THE ULTIMATE WEAPON

A nuclear bomb causes much more than just a huge blast. There is also blinding light, searing heat and lethal radiation that can linger in the environment for hundreds, even thousands of years. 'Fallout' or radioactive dust can then be carried by the wind for hundreds of miles.

EXTREME EXPLOSIONS Nuclear bombs are usually made of uranium or plutonium, which release massive amounts of energy when detonated.

● The worst nuclear disaster took place at Chernobyl's No 4 Reactor in the former USSR (now Ukraine). The official death toll was only 31, but no one knows how many of the 200,000 people involved in the clean-up operation died in the five-year period following the catastrophe.

Shocking nuclear detonations

The most powerful atomic bomb of all was detonated in Russia's arctic island of Novaya Zemlya at 8.33am GMT on 30 October 1961. It was a thermo-nuclear device, with a power of at least 57 megatons, equivalent to 57,000,000 tons of TNT high explosive. Some experts believe that the power of this atomic bomb test was even bigger – closer to 90 megatons. It caused a shock wave that circled the world three times, taking 36 hours 27 minutes for the first circuit. People all over the world felt a slight tremor. No one was killed, but the surrounding area was totally devastated.

UNNATURAL CATASTROPHES

THE SINKING OF THE TITANIC

The most famous marine disaster happened on 14 April 1912, when the then biggest ship in the world, the 'unsinkable' British White Star liner *Titanic,* struck an iceberg. Before they could be rescued, 1,513 passengers and crew drowned in the cold north Atlantic waters.

Perhaps the worst ever environmental disaster occurred in January 1991. During the Gulf War, the Iraqi ruler, Saddam Hussein, tried to halt the allied forces' advance by ordering hundreds of oil wells to be set on fire in southern Iraq and Kuwait. He also ordered 816,000 tonnes of crude oil to be released into the Persian Gulf, causing a huge oil slick, up to 432mm (17in) thick and 644km (400 miles) long.

RED ALERT The brave fire-fighting Texan 'Red' Adair came out of retirement to face the biggest challenge of his life – putting out the raging oil well fires in Kuwait.

PLAGUED BY DEATH

The worst single disaster to have hit mankind is the plague known as the Black Death, which wiped out 75 million people – up to a third of the population in many parts of Asia and Europe – between 1347 and 1351. The disease was carried by rats and passed on to humans by fleas. People then developed bubonic or pneumonic plague from which they usually died within a few days.

WORST TRANSPORT DISASTERS

Almost every day we read or hear news of transport disasters. The worst recorded are:

Sea
About 12,000 people were killed in October 1933 when a gulag transit ship carrying prisoners was crushed in freezing ice packs near Wrangel Island, off Russia.

Road
At least 176 people died when a petrol tanker exploded inside the Salang tunnel, Afghanistan, on 3 November 1982.

Railway
On 6 June 1981, more than 800 passengers died when their train plunged off a bridge into the Bagmati River, in India.

Air
583 people were killed when two Boeing 747s collided at Tenerife airport on 27 March 1977. A Boeing 747 also crashed near Tokyo on 12 August 1985, and 520 died.

DISASTERS IN THE SKIES

Air disasters don't happen very often, but when they do, there is usually a high death toll. When two Boeing 747s collided on the runway at Tenerife, Canary Islands, on 27 March 1977, 583 people were killed, making it the worst air disaster ever.

The worst accident involving only one plane occurred on 12 August 1985, when a JAL Boeing 747 crashed near Tokyo, killing 520 passengers and crew.

The worst terrorist attack happened when a bomb exploded on board an Air India Boeing 747 on 23 June 1985. The plane was so badly damaged it crashed into the Atlantic Ocean off the south-west coast of Ireland – 329 people died.

JINXED JOURNEY A burning DC10 is covered in foam after crashing in Fukuoka, Japan on 13 June 1996.

Fortunately, mid-air collisions are even rarer than other air crashes. The worst one occurred on 12 November 1996; a Kazakh Illyushin-76 collided with a Saudi Boeing 747 near Delhi, in India, killing 351 people.

HITTING THE HEADLINES

Air crashes always make headline news, but it's worth remembering that statistically you are much safer in a plane than when you are crossing the road.

BUILDINGS
AND TRAVEL

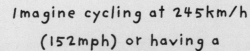
Imagine cycling at 245km/h (152mph) or having a swimming pool in your car!

EXTREME BUILDINGS

People began building really tall structures in about 2,900BC with the first pyramids in Egypt. This century, buildings have been built higher and higher as cities compete to have the tallest 'skyscraper' in the world. Today, the tallest are the twin Petronas Towers in Kuala Lumpur, Malaysia, but even they are being overtaken by the Chongquing Tower in Chungking, China. It will be a dizzy-making 457m (1,499ft) high and have 98 storeys!

THE PETRONAS TOWERS – 451.9M (1,482FT) TALL

The tallest structure ever built was a Polish radio mast, which measured 646.38m (2,120ft). After the 500-tonne tower crashed to the ground, it was jokingly called 'the world's longest structure'.

UP AND UP – ON AND ON

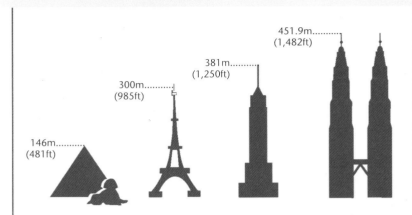

TALLER AND TALLER From left to right: the Great Pyramid at Giza, Egypt, finished in 2,860 BC; the Eiffel Tower in Paris (1889); New York's Empire State Building (1931); and the twin Petronas Towers in Kuala Lumpur, Malaysia (1996).

The earliest known human structure is about 1,700,000 years old. It consists of more than 600 stone blocks placed in a circle, to form the base of a hut in the Olduvai Gorge in Tanzania, east Africa.

BRIDGING A VERY LARGE GAP In April 1998, the Japanese opened the Akashi-Kaikyo suspension bridge, which spans 1,991m (6,532ft) and joins the islands of Honshu and Shikoku.

THE LONGEST BRIDGE IN THE WORLD

LAND SPEED RECORD

The fastest car ever built and the only one ever to pass through the sound barrier is the British-built SSC *Thrust II*. On 15 October 1997, over the Black Rock Desert in Nevada, USA, RAF pilot Andy Green achieved a land speed record of 1,227.98km/h (763mph). The time-keepers and the support crew were led by Richard Noble, the previous land speed record-holder – at 1,019.5km/h (633.47 mph). The whole team heard the supersonic bang as *Thrust II* made automobile history.

The highest speed ever attained by a normal road car is 349.21 km/h (217.1mph) by a Jaguar XJ220. It was driven round the Nardo test track in Italy in 1992 by the racing driver Martin Brundle.

The fastest acceleration by a road car was achieved by a Ford RS200 Evolution in 1994. The driver, Graham Hathaway, shot off from a standing start to reach 96.5 km/h (60 mph) after just 3.07 seconds.

SPEED MACHINE British-built SSC *Thrust II*, driven by RAF pilot Andy Green, is the only car to have broken the sound barrier. It reached 1,227.98 km/h (763.035mph) on 15 October 1997.

In 1974, Roy Rawlins got off with a caution from the Californian police for driving at 152 km/h (95 mph) in a 55 mph zone. What made the incident so extraordinary was that Mr Rawlins was then almost 104 years old! He continued driving until just before his 105th birthday.

THE CAR THAT BROKE THE SOUND BARRIER

EXPENSIVE AND EXPANSIVE

CLASSIC CARS

The most expensive cars in the world are not new ones such as the £440,000 Jaguar XJ220, above, but treasured veterans. Their prices are often secret, but a 1962 Ferrari 250GTO was sold at public auction in Monte Carlo, Monaco on 22 May 1990 for £6.4 million.

Custom-built cars have been stretched up to 30.5m (100ft) in length, but are, of course, quite unable to get around sharp corners. One example, a 'limo' built by Jay Ohrberg from Burbank, California, USA needed 26 wheels. It features a swimming pool – complete with a diving board – a pad for landing a mini-helicopter and a king-sized water-bed! Luckily it can be made to bend in the middle so that it can get round most corners. The record was previously held by a 21.93 m (71ft 11in) Cadillac, which also had a swimming pool!

A LONG DRIVE Some custom-built cars have been stretched to 30.5m (100ft), but parking them can prove to be a real nightmare!

TRANSPORT AND SPEED

The greatest ship ever built was the tanker *Happy Giant*. She was completed at the Nippon Kokan shipyard in January 1981, and has a length of more than a quarter of a mile – 458.45m (1,504ft) at 564,763 tonnes dead-weight. She is so vast that the crew travel from the bow to the stern and back again on bicycles. She was seriously damaged during the Iran-Iraq War in the Persian Gulf, but was refitted in Dubai and Singapore, and relaunched in 1991 with the name *Jahre Viking*. You will not see her in the English Channel, because she is simply too big! She has a draught (depth under water) of 24.6m (81ft) and could not make a safe passage. Imagine something as tall as an eight-storey building ploughing through the water!

The biggest crash of all time happened in 1977, just off the coast of South Africa. The massive oil tanker *Venpet*, which could carry a cargo of 330,869 tonnes, collided with her even larger sister ship *Venoil*, which could carry 330,954 tonnes of oil. There was a lot of explaining to do!

VVVRROOOOOOOMM!

American, Dave Campos rode his 7m (23ft) long motorbike, *Easyriders*, on the Bonneville Salt Flats, Utah, covering 1km every 6.9 seconds, or a mile in under 11 seconds. The highest speed he reached was an incredible 519.61km/h (322.87mph)!

THE WORST DRIVER IN THE WORLD

The title of 'worst driver in the world' appears to have been earned in McKinney, Texas, USA, by a 75-year-old man. On one day – 15 October 1966 – he received ten police tickets for traffic violations. He drove on the wrong side of the road four times, committed four hit-and-run offences and caused five accidents. His sixth accident of the day was his last – he reversed into a police car!

The highest speed ever recorded on a national railway system is 515.3km/h (320.2mph), by the French SNCF high-speed TGV (Train à Grande Vitesse) *Atlantique*, between Courtalain and Tours in 1990.

MOVING AT THE SPEED OF LIGHT

Sometimes the question is asked: 'What is the fastest speed that man has ever made any object move?' Of course, the answer used to be bullets, which reached up to 1,600km/h (1,000mph). However, once rockets were invented, speeds began to climb. The German World War II V2 of 1942-45 reached 5,790km/h (3,598mph). In 1972, the fastest space vehicle so far left the Earth at an amazing 51,682km/h (32,114mph).

PEDAL POWER

Lotus developed a revolutionary bicycle with a one-piece body made from carbon fibre in 1992. The bike helped the British cyclist Chris Boardman win a gold medal in record time at the Barcelona Olympics.

Tiny particles have since been made to move at almost the speed of light – approximately 300,000 km per second or (669,000,000 mph) – in specially built underground tunnels, which appropriately enough are called 'atom smashers' or cynchrotrons.

MONSTER TRUCK The largest dump truck in the world can carry 317.5 tonnes – the weight of ten double-decker buses. When it's tipping, it is the height of a five-storey building!

THE FASTEST BICYCLE

- The highest speed ever attained on a bicycle was achieved by American, John Howard. On 20 July 1985, he pedalled behind the wind shield of his pace-car on Bonneville Salt Flats, Utah, USA, and reached the almost unbelievable speed of 245km/h (152mph)!

39

THE FASTEST IN THE SKIES

The official world air speed record is limited to aircraft which take off under their own power. The American rocket-powered Aviation X-15 A2 attained a speed of 27,274km/h (4,520mph) at very high altitude, but because it was released from a mother plane in October 1967, the feat was never allowed as an aircraft record.

- Only 32 'Blackbirds' were built. They could fly at an altitude of 24,385m (80,000ft) and were used for spying. Two huge Pratt & Whitney turbo ram-jets gave them a top speed of Mach 3.35 – 3.35 times the speed of sound!

A SPEED OF OVER 3,529km/h 2,193mph

The official air speed record was set on 28 July 1976, by a Lockheed SR-71A 'Blackbird', near Beale Air Force Base, California, USA. It was piloted by Captain Eldon W Joersz and Major George T Morgan. Flying over a low-level course, they reached a speed of 3,529km/h (2,193mph). Amazingly, their record has stood for more than 22 years and it's still looking safe!

TURBO-CHARGED The Blackbird's final flight from Los Angeles to Washington DC took a defiant 64 minutes 5 seconds.

EXTREME

ANIMALS AND PLANTS

Find out about a
frog that can
kill 2,830,000
people, and beans
that are 2m
(6ft 7in) long!

SCARY SPIDERS

The world's largest known spiders live in the rain forests of South America and are called goliath bird-eating spiders – for obvious reasons! A male spider caught in Venezuela in April 1965 had a leg-span of 280mm (11in). To eat their prey, some bird-eating spiders have fangs that are 25mm (1in) long! Apart from small birds, they like eating lizards, mice and other small rodents.

The well-known daddy long-legs rarely exceeds 114mm (4½in) in leg-span, but one specimen found in the United Kingdom measured 152mm (6in) across.

The longest lived of all spiders are those that belong to the tarantula family. One adult female collected in Mexico in 1935, lived for 25 years, but no one could tell exactly how old it was when the spider was found.

DEADLY WIDOW

All spiders contain poison that can be used to catch prey, but only a few have venom sufficiently powerful to affect humans. One of the most venomous is the black widow, found in most parts of the world except central Europe and northern Eurasia. It exhibits a red mark on its abdomen as a warning signal and, as its name suggests, the female often kills the male after mating. Its venom acts as a powerful nerve toxin, causing extreme pain, and sometimes even death!

ON THE RUN The fastest spider in the world is the long-legged sun-spider which lives in the semi-desert regions of Africa and the Middle East. It can reach speeds of 16 km/h (10mph) – fast enough to catch all sorts of prey!

A real handful!

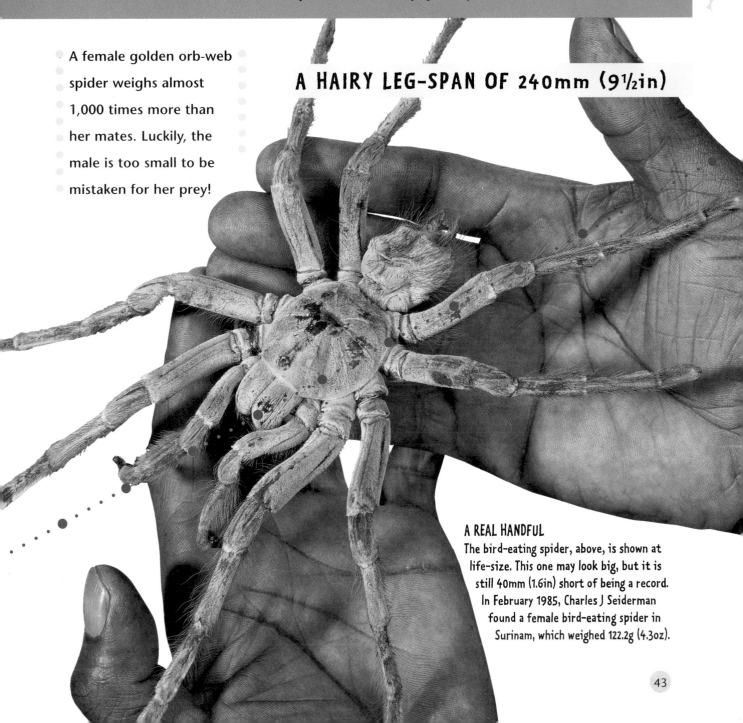

A female golden orb-web spider weighs almost 1,000 times more than her mates. Luckily, the male is too small to be mistaken for her prey!

A HAIRY LEG-SPAN OF 240mm (9½in)

A REAL HANDFUL
The bird-eating spider, above, is shown at life-size. This one may look big, but it is still 40mm (1.6in) short of being a record. In February 1985, Charles J Seiderman found a female bird-eating spider in Surinam, which weighed 122.2g (4.3oz).

43

ANIMAL KILLERS

What is the most poisonous animal? Is it a snake, a frog, a spider, a jellyfish or some other creature? The most venomous snake in the world is the black-headed sea snake, found in the Timor Sea, north of Australia. In 1974, the Japanese scientist, Dr Noburo Tamiya, found that its venom was 100 times more lethal than that of any other sea or land snake.

The most poisonous spider is the Brazilian wandering spider. As little as 0.10mg (0.0000035oz) of its venom will cause total respiratory failure and then death!

QUICK GETAWAY The fastest snake is the black mamba of Africa, which can move faster than many people can run!

SNAKES CAN TRAVEL AT 20km/h (12mph)

FATAL FACT
More people die of snake bites in Sri Lanka than in any other country in the world. On average, snakes kill 800 people on the island each year.

Some snakes, such as this viper, have a heat-sensitive organ midway between each nostril and eye to help them aim their strike at warm-blooded prey.

Venomous encounters

CRUSHING DEFEAT Pythons kill by squeezing their prey between their coils. They have been known to swallow goats, pigs or deer whole – one even killed a 14-year-old Indonesian boy.

The greatest authenticated length for a snake is exactly 10m (32ft 9½in) for a reticulated python, shot on the north coast of the Indonesian island of Celebes in 1912. It was measured by a civil engineer using a surveying tape. Snakes continue growing throughout their lives.

ENOUGH POISON TO KILL 2,830,000 PEOPLE

More deadly than either the black-headed sea snake, or the Brazilian wandering spider, is the kokoi or two-toned arrow-poison frog, which lives in the forests of north-west Colombia in South America. It has been calculated that 28.3g (1oz) of its poison – which is secreted through its skin – would be enough to wipe out a large city of 2,830,000 people!

South American Indians used the venom from arrow-poison frogs to coat their arrow tips. The poison causes muscle cramps, twitching, vomiting, convulsions, paralysis and heart failure – then death.

BEASTS BENEATH THE SEA

Octopuses live in the coastal waters of the north Pacific Ocean. The largest ever recorded was 'wrestled' to the surface by a lone American scuba diver, Donald E Haagen, in 1973.

It had a radial span of 7m (23ft). But even this monster pales into insignificance when compared with the largest squid. In 1878, an Atlantic giant squid ran aground in Newfoundland, eastern

Canada. Its body was 6.1m (20ft) long and one of its mighty tentacles was 10.7m (35ft) long, giving it a span of more than 22.8m (75ft) – that's well over the length of two double-decker buses!

CLOSE ENCOUNTER A diver swims above a giant octopus, 7m (23ft) across. There have been many unconfirmed reports of creatures even bigger than this one.

DID YOU KNOW?

As octopuses go, the blue-ringed octopus is probably the most beautiful. But don't ever touch one. Their poison can kill up to 10 people in only a matter of minutes!

Spectacular specimens

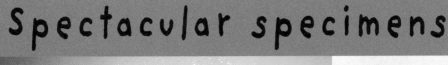

A SPAN OF MORE THAN 7m (23ft)

BIG BLUE The largest of all living animals is the blue whale, found in the colder parts of the oceans. The heaviest ever measured was a female found in 1947; she was 27.6m (90½ft) long and 190 tonnes.

- One of the most spectacular marine creatures is the
- manta ray, which is also called a devil ray because it has
- two horn-like fins coming out of its head. Large specimens
- have spans of 7m (23ft), but there have been reports of
- even larger rays with spans approaching 9m (nearly 30ft).

HARD TO SPOT The most venomous fish in the world is the ugly and carnivorous stonefish. Found in the warm waters of the Indo-Pacific, it camouflages itself and waits for its prey. Contact with its spines stuns other fish immediately and can kill a person within 20 minutes.

Stonefish, found in the warm waters of the Indo-Pacific, are the most venomous fish in the world. The appropriately named *Synanceja horrida* is a particularly poisonous member of the family. Several people have died after treading on its poisonous spines.

The most aggressive fish is probably the piranha. Though small, they can use their razor sharp teeth to terrifying effect, and have claimed hundreds of lives in South America.

NATURAL BORN KILLERS

The largest carnivorous fish is the great white shark, which has many other names, including the man-eater, the blue pointer, the white death shark or the carcharodon. It is believed that specimens which have been gorging themselves on a whale carcass may reach 3.17 tonnes (7,000lb) in weight. In 1829, a specimen 6.7m (22ft) long was caught off the coast of southern France. And it was later reported that the undigested remains of a headless body of a man, in full armour, was found in this huge shark's stomach! The official length and weight record is held by a 6.4m (21ft) female, caught off Cuba in 1945, which weighed in at a whopping 3,313kg (7,303lb).

KILLER JELLYFISH

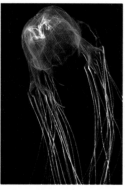

The most dangerous species of jellyfish is the Australian box jellyfish, the sting of which can kill in one to three minutes if medical help is not available. What makes it particularly dangerous is that it is semi-transparent.

THE MOST DEADLY OF OCEAN HUNTERS

- Of the many varieties of jellyfish, the largest by far is the Arctic giant jellyfish of the north-western Atlantic. One was washed up in Massachusetts Bay on the east coast of the United States in 1870. Its 'bell' measured 2.3m (7½ft) across, while its tentacles stretched an amazing 36.5m (120ft) – the length of nine medium-sized cars!

Hungry hunters

LETHAL JAWS There are more than 100 shark attacks in the world each year, a quarter of which are fatal. Sharks tend to strike when they're hungry or harassed, or when someone is bleeding or thrashing about in the water. Man-eating sharks include the great white (above), the hammerhead, blue sharks and tiger sharks (right).

THE FASTEST ON THE PLANET

101km/h (63mph)

The fastest of all land animals is the cheetah from southern and eastern Africa, Iran and Baluchistan. It can reach 101km/h (63mph) – more than twice as fast as Carl Lewis, the fastest ever man. Cheetahs can only run at this speed for short bursts, but that is often all that is needed to catch their prey.

108km/h (67mph)

A fish that can swim faster than a cheetah can run seems impossible. But in 1925, a hooked sailfish was timed as it zipped out to sea from Florida's coast. In exactly three seconds it pulled out 91m (100yds) of line – in other words, it must have been travelling at 108km/h (67mph)!

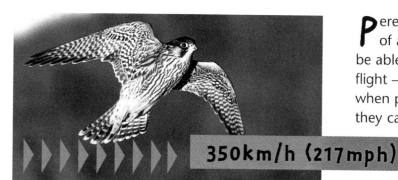

350km/h (217mph)

Peregrine falcons are the fastest moving of all animals. Spine-tailed swifts may be able to fly faster than falcons in level flight – at about 170km/h (106mph) – but when peregrine falcons are diving for prey, they can reach extraordinary speeds. It is estimated that during a 'stoop', or a dive, they can reach speeds of up to 350km/h (217mph)!

THE WIDEST WINGSPAN

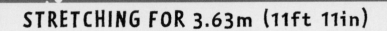

STRETCHING FOR 3.63m (11ft 11in)

Of all the nearly 9,000 different species of bird, the one with the greatest wingspan is the wandering albatross of the southern oceans. In 1965, the American Antarctic research vessel, USNS *Eltanin*, caught a male wandering albatross in the Tasman Sea with an unstretched wingspan of 3.63m (11ft 11in). Earlier records of even greater wingspans are less reliable, but among the total world population of about 50,000, a few must reach more than 3.7m (12ft) from wing tip to wing tip. The 'sail area' of the broad-winged Andean condor is much larger than that of the narrow-winged albatross, but no example has ever been found to have a wingspan of more than 3.15m (10ft 4in).

BIG BIRD Albatrosses can soar for hours without flapping their wings once. The naturalist, David Attenborough, lies beside one of the birds (above right).

The bird which spends most time in the air is the sooty tern. It remains aloft for up to ten years before returning to land to breed. The most aerial land bird is the swift – it sleeps, drinks, eats and even mates in the air!

THE WORLD'S BIGGEST LITTERS

The largest recorded litter of puppies belonged to 'Lena', an American foxhound bitch owned by Commander WN Ely of Ambler, Pennsylvania, USA. She gave birth to 23 puppies on 19 June 1944, all of which survived. The same number was produced by 'Shalimar Bootsie', a Great Dane owned by Marjorie Harris of Little Hall, near Colchester, Essex, in June 1987. In this case, however, only 16 survived.

PUPPY LOVE Of the 6,600,000 dogs in the United Kingdom, one of the most popular breeds is the labrador. These nine golden labrador puppies show why.

HERE KITTY, KITTY, KITTY, KITTY...

SUPERMUMS A tabby named 'Dusty' from Texas, USA, had a total of 420 kittens. The largest single litter was to a Burmese-Siamese cross, who gave birth to 19 kittens, of which 15 survived.

THE EARTH'S TALLEST TREES

Of all living trees, the tallest is a coast redwood growing in Montgomery State Reserve, in California. It measures 112.1m (368ft), making it taller than St Paul's Cathedral in London. The tree is thought to be at least 1,000 years old, but it is still growing!

TRUNK ROADS Some of the sequoia and redwood trees in California are so massive, you can literally drive a car through tunnels made in their trunks.

TALLER THAN ST PAUL'S CATHEDRAL!

TO EAT? OR NOT TO EAT?

EDIBLE GIANTS

In 1996, Nathan and Paula Zehr in Lowville, New York State, USA, grew the first recorded pumpkin which weighed more than half an American ton – 481kg (1,060lb). The world's largest apple was grown by the Hanners family in Oregon, USA, in 1994 – it was 1.47kg (3lb 4oz). The longest 'edible' green beans were 121.9cm (48in) long and grown in North Carolina, USA. Giant, but inedible beans of up to 2m (79in) grow in New Zealand.

• The most deadly of all poisonous fungi is the yellowish-olive death cap mushroom, which can be found in England. If eaten, they can kill within 6 to 15 hours if medical help is not sought quickly. Of its many victims, the most famous was Pope Clement VII. Against all advice, he unwisely tried one in 1534 and died soon afterwards!

EXTREME

SPORT

Find out who ran 300km (186 miles) in a single day and which footballer won the World Cup three times!

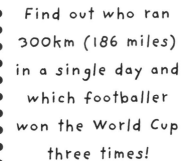

FASTEST AND FURTHEST

Running events that are even longer than the 42.195km (26 miles 385 yards) of a marathon are called ultra-distance events. The world's most successful ultra-distance runner is Yiannis Kouros of Greece who set out to run further than anyone else in a single day.

In October 1997, he finally achieved the aim of all ultra-distance runners – he covered 300km (186 miles 724 yards) within 24 hours. That is the equivalent of running more than seven marathons at an average speed of 12.5km/h (7¾mph) one after another – all day and all night!

Even when Donovan Bailey set a new 100m world record of 9.84 seconds, his top speed was never quite as high as that achieved by Carl Lewis.

GOING FOR GOLD Not only is he the fastest man ever recorded, but Carl Lewis also won a record nine Olympic Gold Medals between 1984 and 1996.

THE FASTEST MAN ON EARTH

- An analysis of the 1988 Olympic 100m final showed that Carl Lewis (right) of the USA reached a speed of 43.37km/h (26.94mph). Canadian, Ben Johnson, achieved exactly the same speed and won the race, but was later stripped of the title after it was found he had been using steroids.

43.37 km/h 26.94 mph

A leap into history

LONG LASTING In 1968, Bob Beamon (above) set a world long jump record, with a leap of 8.9m (29ft 2½in). It was 23 years before Mike Powell (right) set a new record of 8.95m (29ft 4½in).

When Mike Powell set his world record for the long jump, he leapt the length of three smallish cars. Now long jumpers are competing to become the first person to jump 9m (29ft 6½in), or better still, to be the first to reach the magical 30ft-mark!

IMAGINE JUMPING THE LENGTH OF 3 CARS!

0   10   20   30

THE HIGH JUMP

High-jumping is a sport which really shows just how much athletes have improved over the years. The first authenticated jump of more than 1.83m (6ft) was in 1876, when Marshall Brooks cleared the bar at an Oxford University meeting. The clearing of 2.13m (7ft) had to wait 80 years – until 1956 – when Charles Dumas straddled 2.15m (7ft 0⅝in), while qualifying for the US Olympic team. Then in 1993, the 8ft (2.45m) barrier fell to the Cuban, Javier Sotomayor. He cleared an amazing 2.44m (8ft 0⅛in) on 29 July 1989, using the 'Fosbury flop' technique (pictured above).

BREAKING THE BARRIER In July 1993, Javier Sotomayor improved on his own high jump record to clear 2.45m (8ft 0½in) – higher than the ceilings of most rooms!

The lowest height of a bar that anyone has 'limboed' under is just 15.5cm (6⅛in), by Marlene Raymond in 1973. However, an even lower height of 13.3cm (5¼in) – which is roughly the height of a soft drink can – has been achieved by a number of girls who did the splits wearing special roller skates.

AN ATHLETE THE HEIGHT OF A GOALPOST

- The tallest athletes are basketball players, who
- frequently exceed 2.13m (7ft). The tallest on record was
- Suleiman 'Ali' Nashnush, who represented Libya in 1962;
- he measured an awesome 2.45m (8ft 0½in).

BIG AND STRONG

THE 'DUMP TRUCK'!

The heaviest sportsman to date has been a sumo wrestler, Salevaa Fuali Atisanoe, alias Konishiki or the 'Dump Truck'. At a competition in Tokyo, in 1994, he weighed in at 267kg (42st 1lb)!

However, the greatest weight ever raised by a human is 2.844 tonnes (6,270lb) in a back lift (in which the weight is raised off steel props) by the 165kg (26 stone) American, Paul Anderson, as long ago as 1957. It is the equivalent of getting underneath a large Rolls-Royce and lifting it up!

LIFT OFF In 1996, Andrei Chemerkin (below) lifted 260kg (573lb) – very nearly the weight of the 'Dump Truck' (left) – above his head, to set a new world record.

Weightlifting has been an Olympic sport ever since the Games were revived in Athens, Greece, in 1896. The event in which the heaviest weights are lifted from the floor to an overhead position is called the clean and jerk. In the 'super-heavyweight' class – for men with a bodyweight of more than 108kg (17 stone), the great barrier had long been 250kg (550lb). This was at last achieved by Aleksandr Kurlovich of Belarus in 1994. The American, Lamar Grant, became the first man to deadlift five times his own body weight in 1985.

BIG HITTERS

The world's fastest ball game is the Basque sport of *pelota vasca* or *jaï alaï*, in which the ball is propelled from a curved wicker basket strapped on to the player's arm. A speed of 302km/h (188mph) has been recorded. This compares to the fastest serve in tennis by Greg Rusedski at a little under 241.4km/h (150mph) and just under 160.9km/h (100mph) for the fastest ball bowled in cricket, by Jeffrey Thomson. The fastest baseball pitcher was Lynn Nolan Ryan for the California Angels who, on 20 August 1974, pitched at 162.3km/h (100.9mph).

- In golf, the longest ever hole-in-one was achieved by Robert Mitera at the 408m (446yds) tenth hole at the Miracle Hills Golf Club, Nebraska, USA, on 7 October 1965.

ENTER 'THE DON' The Australian batsman, Donald Bradman was known for his quick eye and his nimble footwork. In 1930, he set a record of 974 runs in a Test series against England. His record still stands today – 68 years later.

A GOOD INNINGS Brian Lara (above) holds the record for the highest ever first-class score. Playing for Warwickshire against Durham at Edgbaston, Birmingham, in 1994, he made 501 not out in less than 8 hours of play!

THE GREATEST EVER BATSMAN?

Australian cricketer, Sir Donald Bradman, known as 'the Don', is regarded by many as the greatest batsman of all time. During his career, which lasted from 1927 to 1948, he scored 28,067 first-class runs at an average of 95.14. And in Test matches, he made 6,996 runs at an even higher average of 99.94. Both of these are still world records, 50 years later.

FOOTBALLING HEROES

RISING STAR When he played against Chile on 11 February 1998, Michael Owen (right) became the youngest footballer this century to make his England debut – at 18 years 58 days. He then went on to score one of the finest goals in the 1998 World Cup.

The Brazilian footballer, Edson Arantes do Nascimento, alias Pelé (left), is widely regarded as being the greatest footballer of all time. He scored an amazing 77 goals in 92 internationals, helping Brazil win three World Cups. Pelé now helps to coach the American football team.

THREE WORLD CUP WINNERS' MEDALS

INDEX

FOOTBALLING HEROES

RISING STAR When he played against Chile on 11 February 1998, Michael Owen (right) became the youngest footballer this century to make his England debut – at 18 years 58 days. He then went on to score one of the finest goals in the 1998 World Cup.

The Brazilian footballer, Edson Arantes do Nascimento, alias Pelé (left), is widely regarded as being the greatest footballer of all time. He scored an amazing 77 goals in 92 internationals, helping Brazil win three World Cups. Pelé now helps to coach the American football team.

THREE WORLD CUP WINNERS' MEDALS

INDEX

ACKNOWLEDGEMENTS

Allsport: p36-37, cover TL p59, BR p61, TR and p55, BR p61, BL p60, TR p57, TL

Ardea: p44 p45, TL and TR p54, TR p51, TC p53, BL

Bruce Coleman Collection: p23, TL and cover 2nd BL and p19, BL p46, BL p50, TL p52, BC

Coloursport: p57, R p55, BL and p59, TL

Corbis: p7, R and p8-9 C

Corbis Bettmann: p20, BL p30, R

Gamma/Frank Spooner Pictures: p9, BL and cover CL and p7, BC

Hulton Getty Collection: p8, BL p12, TL p20, TR p24, BL p26, T p27, TL and TR and p19, BR p30, TL (news vendor)

Image Bank: p52, TR

John Frost Historical Newspaper Loan Service: p31, p32

Mary Evans Picture Library: p30, TL (Titanic)

Michael Gunton: p51, CR

Natural History Museum: p43, C

NHPA: p47, TR p49, TC p50, BL

Oxford Scientific Films: p50, CL

Photonica: p46-49, background

Photoreporters/Corbis: p17, TL and p7, L and TC

Planet Earth Pictures: p22, B p24, BL p42, BL and TR and p41, TR p46, BR p47, BC p48, BL

Popperfoto: p60, CR p56, BR

Popperfoto/Reuter: p14, TL p21, TR and B p54, BL

Rex Features: p13, BL p15, BL-BR p16, BL and TR p17, TR p18, TR and BL p30, BR p32, TR p37, CR and p33, BR p37, TL p36, TR p38, BL p39, BL and TR p40, BC and p33, TR p54, CR and BC

Robert Harding: p28, TR p29, BR cover 2nd TL and p33, BL and p34, L p35, B

Science Photo Library: p40, R

Sporting Pictures: p55, TR and p58, TR

Tony Stone Images: p23, BR p27, BR p25 p47, TL p49, BR p53, R and p41, BL

Abbreviations: T = Top; B = Bottom; L = Left; C = Centre; R = Right.

Picture research by Jane Lambert

OTHER BOOKS IN THIS SERIES:

**The Book of Animals • The Body Book
The Book of Time and Space**